THE PICTURE

The City of Leeds

by

DAVID THORNTON

D&J THORNTON
101 Blue Hill Lane, Leeds
LS12 4NX

DURING THE ICE AGES, ANIMALS LIKE THE MAMMOTH * ROAMED THE VALLEY OF THE RIVER AIRE.

IN WARMER TIMES THE HIPPOPOTAMUS *, THE WILD OX OR AUROCH* AND THE RED DEER INHABITED THE DISTRICT.

Antlers of red deer found at Kirkstall

THE BRONZE AGE PEOPLE WERE KNOWN AS THE *BEAKER PEOPLE* ** AFTER THE FINE POTTERY THEY MADE.

ONE SUCH BEAKER WAS FOUND AT TINSHILL. BRONZE AGE IMPLEMENTS HAVE BEEN DISCOVERED AT ROUNDHAY AND HUNSLET.

AT COOKRIDGE AND IRELAND WOOD THE REMAINS OF IRON AGE HUTS HAVE BEEN FOUND..

.... AND AN IRON AGE FORT IS THOUGHT TO HAVE BEEN ESTABLISHED ON WOODHOUSE MOOR.

ALL TRACES OF IT HAVE NOW DISAPPEARED BUT A ROAD NEARBY STILL RETAINS THE NAME *RAMPART ROAD*.

Roman *amphora* - wine jar - found at Adel

Roman coin found at Headingley

THE ROMANS CREATED A SETTLEMENT AT ADEL - *BURGODONUM* - TO OVERSEE THE BRIGANTES WHO LIVED IN THE AREA.

THERE IS STRONG EVIDENCE TO BELIEVE THE ROMAN FORT, *CAMBODONUM*, WAS SITED AT QUARRY HILL. THE TADCASTER-MANCHESTER ROAD RAN JUST TO THE EAST OF BRIGGATE.

* Fossil remains found at Wortley in 1852

** see *Picture Story of Prehistoric and Roman Yorkshire*

c 730 A.D.
THE FIRST ACTUAL MENTION OF LEEDS OCCURS IN BEDE'S *HISTORY OF THE ENGLISH CHURCH AND PEOPLE*. HE CALLS IT *LOIDIS*.

A church was built at the royal country-seat of Campodunum but this, together with all the other buildings, was burned by the pagans who killed King Edwin, and later kings replaced this seat by another in the vicinity of Loidis. The stone altar of this church survived the fire and is preserved in the monastery that lies in Elmete Wood.

BEDE ALSO DESCRIBES HOW THE PAGAN KING PENDA WAS KILLED AT THE BATTLE of WINWAED ON 15TH NOV. 655 A.D. *IN THE REGION OF LOIDIS*

DURING THE VIKING OCCUPATION YORKSHIRE WAS DIVIDED INTO *RIDINGS* AND THESE WERE THEN DIVIDED INTO *WAPENTAKES*.

Anglian Cross from Leeds Parish Church

The Shire Oak in the early 20th Century

LEEDS WAS IN THE *SKYRACK* WAPENTAKE SAID TO MEET AT THE SHIRE OAK TREE AT HEADINGLEY.

FROM THE BEGINNING OF THE 9TH CENTURY LEEDS HAD A CHURCH OF SOME IMPORTANCE ...

--- AND FROM THE *DOMESDAY BOOK* OF 1086 WE HAVE AN ACCURATE DESCRIPTION OF WHAT *LEDES* WAS LIKE. IT HAD A PRIEST, A CHURCH, A MILL AND ---

One of the two volumes of Domesday Book. They were bound in Tudor Times.

--- 7 THANES - IMPORTANT LANDOWNERS; 27 *VILLEINS* - WHO WERE OBLIGED TO WORK ON THEIR LORD'S LAND AS WELL AS THEIR OWN; AND 4 *BORDARS* - OWNERS OF SMALL PLOTS.

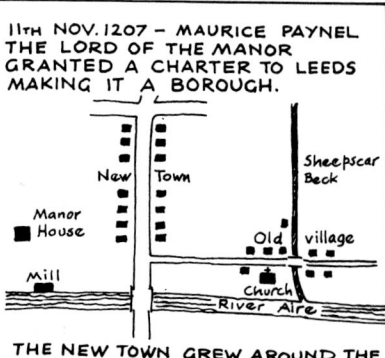

* The Scarborough Hotel near City Square stands on its site.

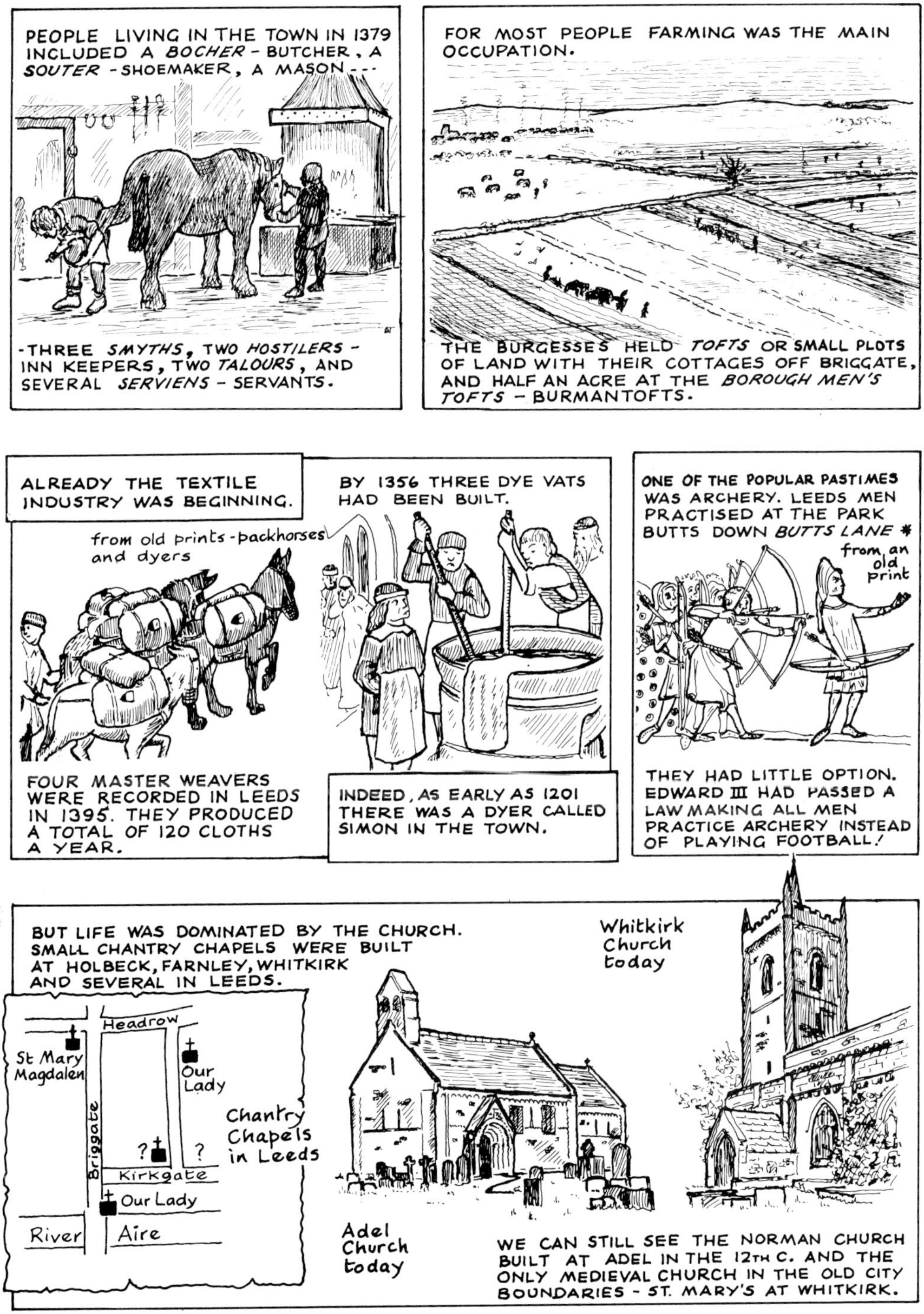

PEOPLE LIVING IN THE TOWN IN 1379 INCLUDED A *BOCHER* - BUTCHER, A *SOUTER* - SHOEMAKER, A MASON --- THREE *SMYTHS*, TWO *HOSTILERS* - INN KEEPERS, TWO *TALOURS*, AND SEVERAL *SERVIENS* - SERVANTS.

FOR MOST PEOPLE FARMING WAS THE MAIN OCCUPATION.

THE BURGESSES HELD *TOFTS* OR SMALL PLOTS OF LAND WITH THEIR COTTAGES OFF BRIGGATE, AND HALF AN ACRE AT THE *BOROUGH MEN'S TOFTS* - BURMANTOFTS.

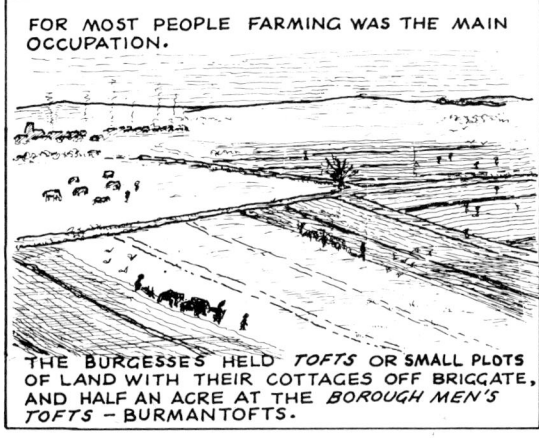

ALREADY THE TEXTILE INDUSTRY WAS BEGINNING.

from old prints - packhorses and dyers

FOUR MASTER WEAVERS WERE RECORDED IN LEEDS IN 1395. THEY PRODUCED A TOTAL OF 120 CLOTHS A YEAR.

BY 1356 THREE DYE VATS HAD BEEN BUILT.

INDEED, AS EARLY AS 1201 THERE WAS A DYER CALLED SIMON IN THE TOWN.

ONE OF THE POPULAR PASTIMES WAS ARCHERY. LEEDS MEN PRACTISED AT THE PARK BUTTS DOWN *BUTTS LANE* *

from an old print

THEY HAD LITTLE OPTION. EDWARD III HAD PASSED A LAW MAKING ALL MEN PRACTICE ARCHERY INSTEAD OF PLAYING FOOTBALL!

BUT LIFE WAS DOMINATED BY THE CHURCH. SMALL CHANTRY CHAPELS WERE BUILT AT HOLBECK, FARNLEY, WHITKIRK AND SEVERAL IN LEEDS.

Chantry Chapels in Leeds

St Mary Magdalen — Headrow — Our Lady — Briggate — Kirkgate — Our Lady — River Aire

Whitkirk Church today

Adel Church today

WE CAN STILL SEE THE NORMAN CHURCH BUILT AT ADEL IN THE 12TH C. AND THE ONLY MEDIEVAL CHURCH IN THE OLD CITY BOUNDARIES - ST. MARY'S AT WHITKIRK.

* Now Basinghall Street

RELIGIOUS SETTLEMENTS WERE ALSO ESTABLISHED IN THE AREA.

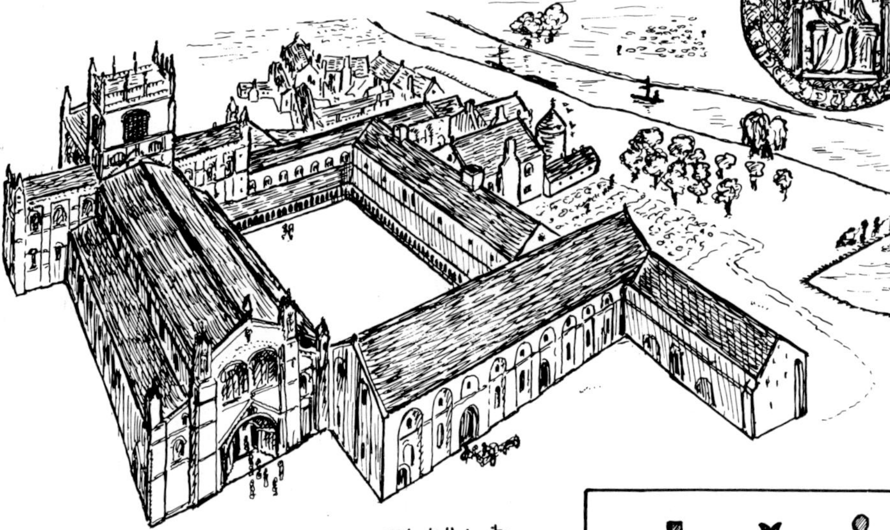

13th Century Seal of Kirkstall Abbey

Kirkstall in its final years.

19TH MAY 1152 - CISTERCIAN MONKS FROM FOUNTAINS ABBEY TOOK OVER THE SMALL RELIGIOUS SETTLEMENT AT *KIRKESTALL*. HERE THEY BUILT THE *MONASTERY OF HEADINGLEY* DEDICATED TO THE VIRGIN MARY. THE MONKS EXPORTED WOOL TO ITALY AND FRANCE. THEIR MONASTERY WAS DISSOLVED IN 1539. *

FROM 1155 UNTIL 1310 THE KNIGHTS TEMPLAR OCCUPIED A SETTLEMENT AT NEWSAM. NOTHING OF THIS REMAINS EXCEPT ITS NAME - *TEMPLENEWSAM*.

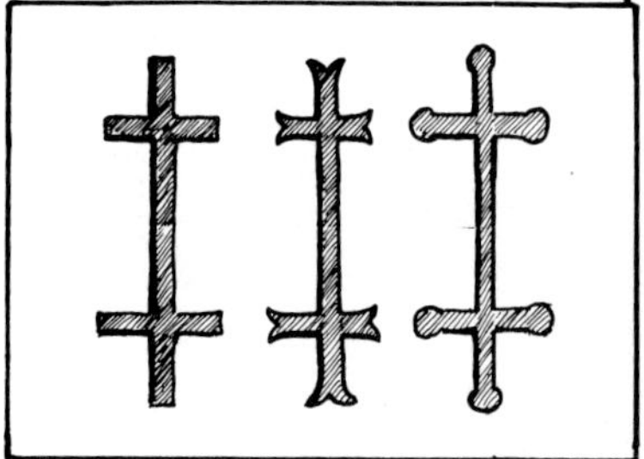

Templar crosses found on buildings in Nether Row. **

THE FIRST DESCRIPTION OF 16TH C. *LEDIS* COMES FROM JOHN LELAND IN THE 1530'S.

Ledis, two miles lower than Christal Abbay on Aire river, is a praty market having one paroche chirche reasonably well buildid and as large as Bradeford but not so quick as it.

BY 1560 WE HAVE THE FIRST MAP OF LEEDS - DRAWN TO SETTLE A DISPUTE OVER MILL RIGHTS.

* see The Picture Story of Kirkstall Abbey   ** Now Lower Headrow

DURING THE REIGN OF JAMES I, LEEDS BECAME A *STAPLE* TOWN. ONLY IN THESE TOWNS COULD WOOL BE SOLD.

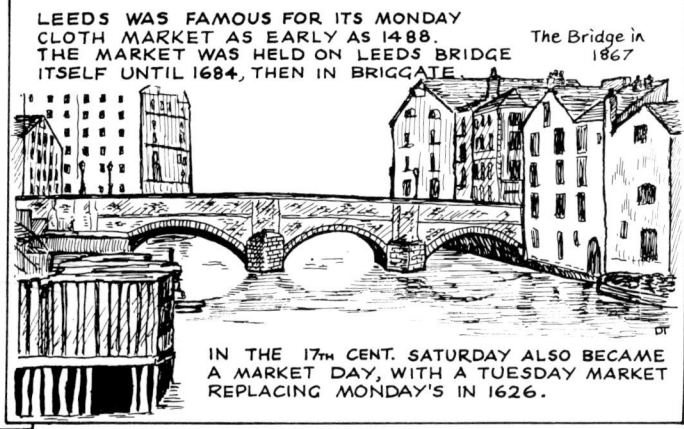

LEEDS WAS FAMOUS FOR ITS MONDAY CLOTH MARKET AS EARLY AS 1488. THE MARKET WAS HELD ON LEEDS BRIDGE ITSELF UNTIL 1684, THEN IN BRIGGATE.

The Bridge in 1867

IN THE 17TH CENT. SATURDAY ALSO BECAME A MARKET DAY, WITH A TUESDAY MARKET REPLACING MONDAY'S IN 1626.

This copy of the charter was made in 1646.

BY THE 1620'S DISHONEST TRADERS WERE DAMAGING THE REPUTATION OF LEEDS CLOTHIERS.

We have willed.. that the aforesaid town of Leedes.. shall from henceforth for ever, be and remain a free borough.. known by the name of the BOROUGH OF LEEDES IN THE COUNTY OF YORK. And that all.. the inhabitants shall be a body corporate and politic.

IN AN EFFORT TO RAISE STANDARDS KING CHARLES I WAS ASKED FOR A TOWN CHARTER.

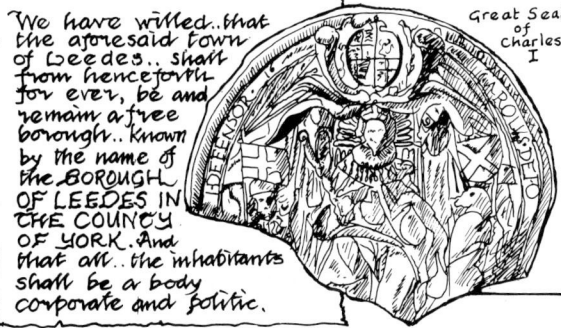

Great Seal of Charles I

13TH JULY 1626 - THIS WAS GRANTED AND NOW A CORPORATION GOVERNED LEEDS.

ONE OF THE MEN WHO CAMPAIGNED FOR THIS WAS JOHN HARRISON, A BRIGGATE CLOTHIER.

HARRISON DID MUCH TO HELP THE TOWN, BUILDING A NEW GRAMMAR SCHOOL IN 1624, ALMSHOUSES AND ST. JOHN'S CHURCH IN 1634.

DURING STUART TIMES LEEDS HAD ITS SHARE OF TROUBLES.

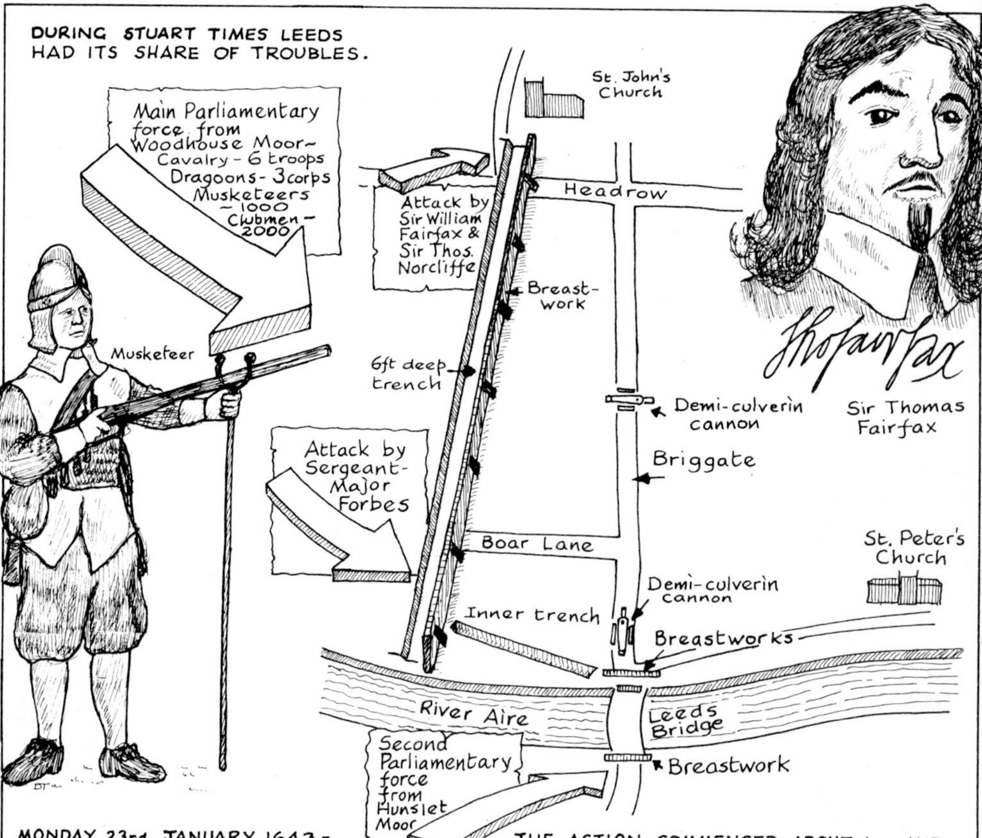

Main Parliamentary force from Woodhouse Moor — Cavalry - 6 troops, Dragoons - 3 corps, Musketeers - 1000, Clubmen - 2000

Musketeer

Attack by Sergeant-Major Forbes

St. John's Church

Headrow

Attack by Sir William Fairfax & Sir Thos. Norcliffe

Breastwork

6ft deep trench

Demi-culverin cannon

Briggate

Boar Lane

Inner trench

Demi-culverin cannon

Breastworks

River Aire

Leeds Bridge

Second Parliamentary force from Hunslet Moor

Breastwork

St. Peter's Church

Sir Thomas Fairfax

MONDAY 23rd JANUARY 1643 — SIR THOMAS FAIRFAX LED A PARLIAMENTARY ARMY AGAINST THE ROYALIST HELD TOWN.

THE ACTION COMMENCED ABOUT 1pm AND LASTED 2 HOURS. FAIRFAX TOOK 500 PRISONERS AND WROTE — *THERE WERE NOT ABOVE 40 SLAIN.*

BUBONIC PLAGUE RAVAGED THE POPULATION FROM MARCH TO DECEMBER 1645 1,325 PEOPLE DIED.

The flea carried by the black rat spread the disease.

THE OUTBREAK BEGAN IN *VICAR LAINE* BUT SOON SPREAD TO WORTLEY, *HOULBECK*, ARMLEY, WOODHOUSE AND OTHER PLACES.

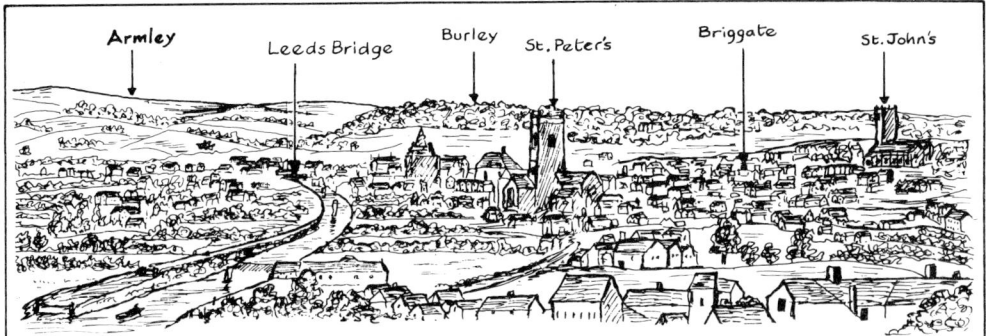

Armley — Leeds Bridge — Burley — St. Peter's — Briggate — St. John's

BY THE LATE 17TH C. AND EARLY 18TH C. LEEDS STILL COVERED A FAIRLY SMALL AREA. THE MOST IMPORTANT HOUSES WERE IN BRIGGATE, *BORE LANE*, KIRKGATE AND CALL LANE. THE CALLS WAS AN OPEN SPACE WITH ORCHARDS. WEST OF BRIGGATE WERE GARDENS AND A BOWLING GREEN.

WE KNOW ABOUT THIS PERIOD THROUGH RALPH THORESBY, THE FIRST LEEDS HISTORIAN. *

IN HIS *DUCATUS LEODIENSIS* HE DESCRIBES MOOT HALL WHICH STOOD IN BRIGGATE. HERE THE CORPORATION MET. TO ITS RIGHT WAS THE SHAMBLES.

Based on a stained glass window in St. John's Church

HE MENTIONS THE PARISH CROSS WHICH STOOD HIGHER UP THE SAME STREET AND..

.HE TELLS OF PLACES HE VISITED LIKE *GYPTON WELL* — A BATH-HOUSE-IN GLEDHOW VALLEY ROAD.

AT HIS KIRKGATE HOME HE ESTABLISHED A FAMOUS MUSEUM.

SADLY, ON HIS DEATH IT WAS DISBANDED.

* His name lives on in the Thoresby Soc. and Ralph Thoresby High School.

WE CAN FIND OUT A GOOD DEAL ABOUT 18TH CENTURY LEEDS FROM—

 Vol 2. Numb. 29.

The Leeds Mercury:
BEING
The freshest Advices,
FOREIGN and DOMESTICK.

THE *LEEDS MERCURY* FOUNDED IN 1718 AND THE *LEEDES INTELLIGENCER* FOUNDED IN 1754, AND CALLED NOW THE *YORKSHIRE POST*.

MUSIC AND DANCING TOOK PLACE AT THE *ASSEMBLY ROOMS* WHILST DRAMA WAS PERFORMED AT TATE WILKINSON'S *THEATRE ROYAL* ON HUNSLET LANE. MUSIC HALLS OPENED IN ALBION STREET & VICAR LANE.

1727 — TRINITY CHURCH BECAME THE THIRD ANGLICAN CHURCH IN THE TOWN.

Apparatus used by Priestley in his experiments

AMONG THE NON-CONFORMISTS WERE THE UNITARIANS AT MILL HILL CHAPEL. THE MINISTER HERE, FROM 1767-73, WAS THE SCIENTIST, JOSEPH PRIESTLEY. IT WAS IN AUGUST 1774 THAT HE DISCOVERED THE GAS, OXYGEN.

ANOTHER WELL KNOWN FIGURE TO VISIT LEEDS WAS JOHN WESLEY. HE WAS ATTACKED THERE IN 1745 AND 1746. HOWEVER, HE RETURNED IN TRIUMPH IN 1781 TO PREACH TO SOME 1,100 PEOPLE.

John Wesley

TO CATER FOR THE SICK THE *GENERAL INFIRMARY* WAS OPENED ON INFIRMARY STREET IN MARCH 1771.

SERVANTS AT THE HOSPITAL HAD TO BE UNMARRIED AND CHILDREN UNDER 6 WERE NOT ADMITTED — EXCEPT FOR *FRACTURES* OR SOME SURGICAL OPERATION.

1755 — STREET LIGHTING WAS INTRODUCED TO PREVENT *BURGLARIES, ROBBERIES & OTHER OUTRAGES.*

OIL LAMPS WERE USED.

EARLY 18TH C. LEEDS HAD A POPULATION OF ABOUT 11,000* MANY OF THESE DEPENDED ON THE WOOLLEN INDUSTRY FOR THEIR LIVING AND OPEN SPACES WERE SET ASIDE IN THE TOWN WHERE CLOTH COULD BE STRETCHED AND DRIED ON TENTER FRAMES.

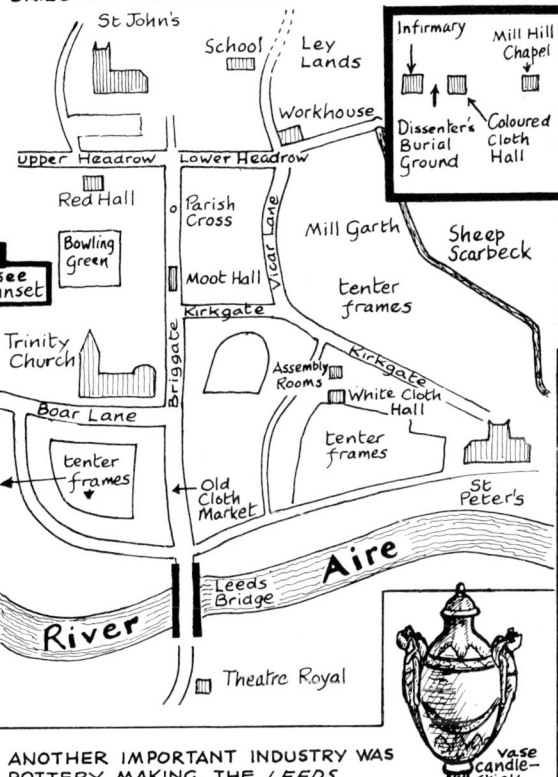

Coloured Cloth Hall in the 1880's

UNDYED CLOTH WAS SOLD AT THE *WHITE CLOTH HALL* WHILST COLOURED OR MIXED CLOTH WAS SOLD AT THE *COLOURED CLOTH HALL* WHICH STOOD WHERE CITY SQUARE IS TODAY.

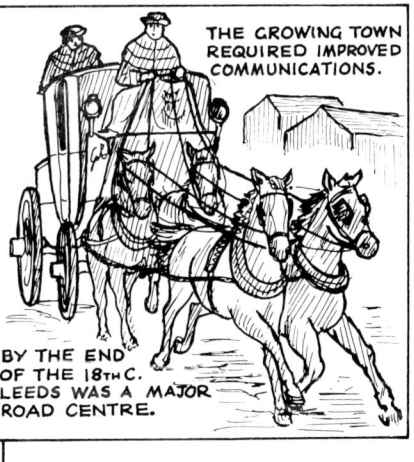

THE GROWING TOWN REQUIRED IMPROVED COMMUNICATIONS.

BY THE END OF THE 18TH C. LEEDS WAS A MAJOR ROAD CENTRE.

ANOTHER IMPORTANT INDUSTRY WAS POTTERY MAKING. THE *LEEDS POTTERY* IN JACK LANE PRODUCED WORLD FAMOUS *CREAM-WARE*.

vase candle-stick

TRANSPORT BY WATER WAS ALSO DEVELOPED. IN 1698 THE AIRE AND CALDER RIVERS WERE MADE NAVIGABLE SO THAT GOODS COULD BE CARRIED MORE EASILY TO HULL.

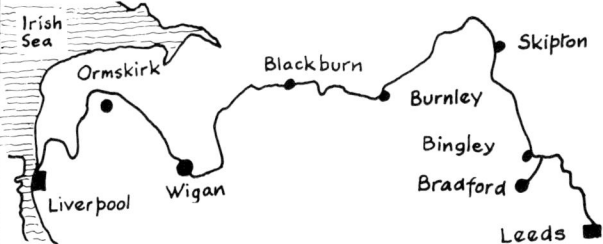

IN 1770 AN ACT OF PARLIAMENT ALLOWED THE BUILDING OF A CANAL THAT WAS TO RUN *FROM LEEDS BRIDGE ... TO ... LIVERPOOLE*. THE CANAL WAS COMPLETED IN 1816.

PERHAPS THE MOST IMPORTANT EVENT TOOK PLACE IN 1758 WHEN THE FIRST EVER RAILWAY ACT OF PARLIAMENT WAS PASSED.

THIS PERMITTED A RAILWAY- OR *WAGGONWAY*-TO BE BUILT BETWEEN MIDDLETON COLLIERY AND *THE GREAT BRIDGE AT LEEDS*. **

* 6,000 in Leeds plus some 5,000 in the nearby villages like Holbeck, Armley & Bramley etc.

** see The Picture Story of Middleton Railway

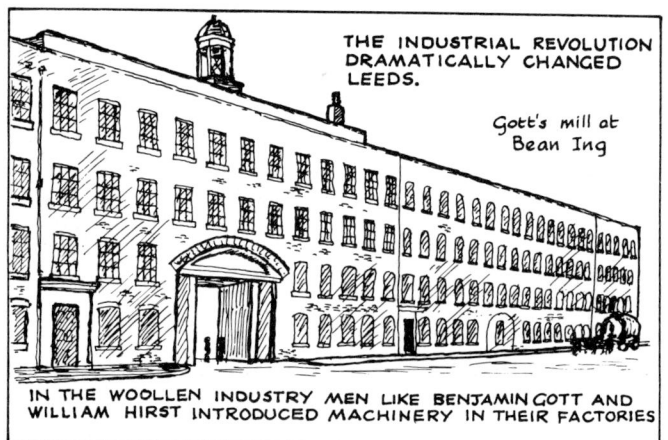

THE INDUSTRIAL REVOLUTION DRAMATICALLY CHANGED LEEDS.

Gott's mill at Bean Ing

IN THE WOOLLEN INDUSTRY MEN LIKE BENJAMIN GOTT AND WILLIAM HIRST INTRODUCED MACHINERY IN THEIR FACTORIES.

FROM 1788 - 1886 LINEN MANUFACTURE WAS ALSO IMPORTANT TO THE TOWN.

Inside Marshall's flax mill - 1843

THEN IN 1855 CAME THE INDUSTRY FOR WHICH LEEDS IS BEST KNOWN ~ READY-MADE CLOTHING

One of the original Singer sewing machines

JOHN BARRAN, USING ISAAC MERRITT SINGER'S NEWLY DEVELOPED SEWING-MACHINE, BEGAN MAKING READY-MADE CLOTHES IN A SMALL FACTORY IN ALFRED STREET.

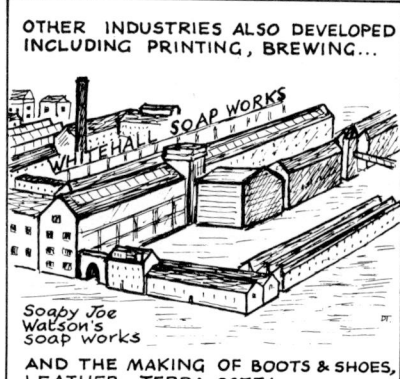

OTHER INDUSTRIES ALSO DEVELOPED INCLUDING PRINTING, BREWING...

Soapy Joe Watson's soap works

AND THE MAKING OF BOOTS & SHOES, LEATHER, TERRA COTTA, COCOA AND SOAP.

WITHOUT DOUBT, ENGINEERING WAS ALSO IMPORTANT TO THE TOWN.

Salamanca - Murray's steam engine built for Middleton Colliery in 1812.

Linden - The first Hunslet Engine Co. locomotive - 1865

MATTHEW MURRAY DEVELOPED THE INDUSTRY AT HIS ROUND FOUNDRY IN HOLBECK.

THROUGH THE 19TH CENTURY ENGINEERING FIRMS EXPANDED AND SOON THEIR GOODS WERE EXPORTED ALL OVER THE WORLD.

THE DEVELOPMENT OF INDUSTRIES IN LEEDS LED TO A LARGE INCREASE IN THE TOWN'S POPULATION. MOST OF THESE NEWCOMERS CAME FROM THE TOWNS AND VILLAGES OF YORKSHIRE. BETWEEN 1841 AND 1851 A LARGE NUMBER OF IRISH SETTLED THERE, AND AFTER 1881 MANY RUSSIAN JEWS ARRIVED.

Leeds about 1846 from Halifax New Road

Population	1801 – 53,162	1841 – 151,874	1881 – 308,628
	1821 – 83,796	1861 – 206,881	1901 – 428,572

HOUSING CONDITIONS WERE OFTEN VERY POOR. JAMES SMITH WROTE IN 1845—

THE MOST UNHEALTHY..YARDS..ARE ONE MASS OF DAMP AND FILTH... THE PRIVIES REMAIN WITHOUT THE REMOVAL..OF THE FILTH FOR 6 MONTHS.

OUTBREAKS OF TYPHUS & CHOLERA STRUCK. BETWEEN JUNE & OCTOBER 1848 SOME 2000 PEOPLE DIED FROM CHOLERA. MOST OF THE VICTIMS LIVED IN MARSH LANE, QUARRY HILL, NEWTOWN & THE LEYLANDS. MEN LIKE ROBERT BAKER, THE MEDICAL OFFICER, CAMPAIGNED TO IMPROVE THINGS. THE *LEEDS IMPROVEMENT ACT* OF 1842 WAS AT LEAST A BEGINNING.

ANOTHER GREAT CAMPAIGNER WHO WAS ACTUALLY BORN IN LEEDS WAS RICHARD OASTLER.

KNOWN AS THE *FACTORY KING*, HE FOUGHT TO IMPROVE THE WORKING CONDITIONS OF CHILDREN IN INDUSTRY.

MANY CHILDREN AT THIS TIME WORKED FROM 5A.M TO 9 P.M.

ONE PATH FROM GOTT'S ARMLEY MILL WAS KNOWN AS *LANTERN LANE.*

Old Wortley Grammar School in 1969.

OTHER CHILDREN WERE MORE FORTUNATE AND ATTENDED THE *TOWN* SCHOOLS AT HEADINGLEY, BEESTON, HOLBECK & WORTLEY.

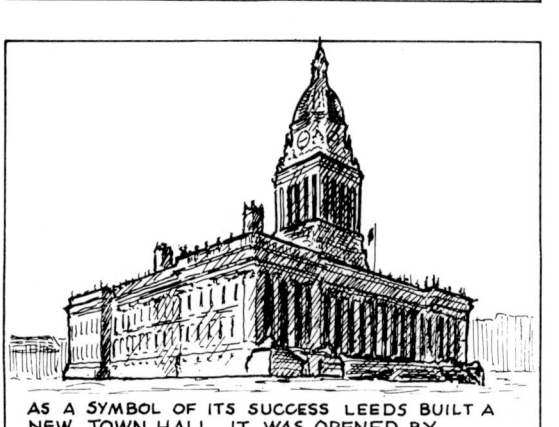
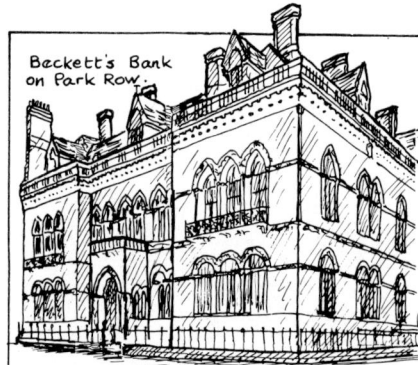

*Leeds became a city in 1893

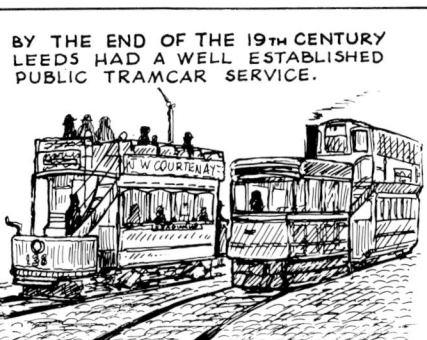

BY THE END OF THE 19TH CENTURY LEEDS HAD A WELL ESTABLISHED PUBLIC TRAMCAR SERVICE.

HORSE TRAMS WERE INTRODUCED IN 1871. STEAM TRAMS FOLLOWED AND IN 1897, ELECTRIC ONES.

IT BECAME ONE OF THE NORTH'S FINEST SHOPPING CENTRES. IT'S ARCADES BECAME EXTREMELY WELL KNOWN — AS IN TIME DID MARK'S *PENNY BAZAAR* IN LEEDS MARKET. *

CHILDREN ATTENDED THE NEW *BOARD SCHOOLS* WHILST AT HOME THEY PLAYED GAMES.

THE BOYS OFTEN PLAYED *PIGGY*, THE GIRLS WITH WOODEN HOOPS CALLED *BOWLERS*. KITES WERE MADE FROM OLD NEWSPAPERS

FOR ENTERTAINMENT, ADULTS VISITED THEATRES, LISTENED TO BANDS IN THE PARKS AND FROM 1890 WATCHED CRICKET AT HEADINGLEY.

1891 - YORKSHIRE'S FIRST GAME THERE WAS LOST!
1899 - FIRST TEST MATCH ON THE GROUND SAW ENGLAND AND AUSTRALIA DRAW - BECAUSE OF RAIN!

SOME OF THE FAMOUS MEN OF VICTORIAN LEEDS.

EDWARD BAINES — EDITOR OF *LEEDS MERCURY*

SIR CLIFFORD ALLBUTT - LEEDS INFIRMARY PHYSICIAN AND INVENTOR OF THE CLINICAL THERMOMETER

DR. W.F. HOOK - VICAR OF LEEDS

PHIL MAY — INTERNATIONAL CARTOONIST.

Eventually became Marks & Spencers *

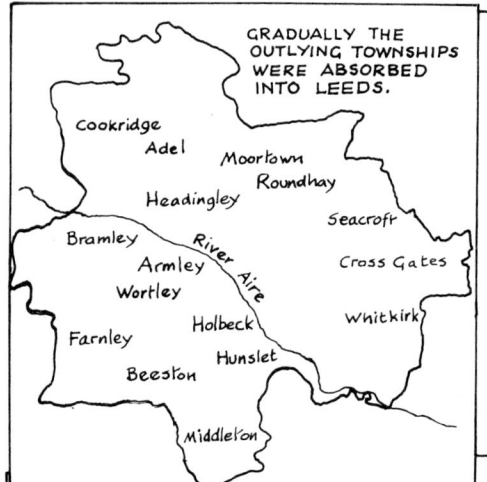

GRADUALLY THE OUTLYING TOWNSHIPS WERE ABSORBED INTO LEEDS.

City Square - opened in 1903

IN 1896 LEEDS WAS DESCRIBED AS A VAST BUSINESS PLACE... A MINIATURE LONDON, AND BOAR LANE AND BRIGGATE IS NEARLY AS BUSY AS LONDON BRIDGE — YORKSHIRE FACTORY TIMES

AN INCREASE IN TRAFFIC LED TO AUTOMATIC TRAFFIC CONTROLS BEING INTRODUCED.

16TH MARCH 1928 - BRITAIN'S FIRST PERMANENT TRAFFIC LIGHTS WERE INSTALLED AT THE JUNCTION OF PARK ROW AND BOND STREET.

BETWEEN 1934 AND 1939 A BOLD SCHEME REMOVED MANY OF THE SLUMS IN THE CITY.

NEW HOUSING ESTATES WERE ESTABLISHED. IN 1938 THE FIRST SECTION OF QUARRY HILL FLATS WAS OPENED. THE FLATS FINALLY PROVIDED 938 HOMES.

LEEDS WAS FORTUNATE IN AVOIDING MUCH DESTRUCTION IN WORLD WAR II - BUT.....

..14TH MARCH 1941 - ITS WORST AIR RAID SAW OVER 60 PEOPLE KILLED, AND SOME 4,600 HOUSES AND THE TOWN HALL DAMAGED.

IN 1974 LEEDS BECAME A METROPOLITAN DISTRICT OF SOME 730,000 PEOPLE....

A FAR CRY FROM THE VILLAGE BEDE DESCRIBED OVER 1,200 YEARS AGO.

We are grateful to the Local History Department of Leeds Ref. Library.